More praise for Carmel L. Morse:

"Each poem in Carmel Morse's debut collection, *Bloodroot,* opens fully in the sun of memory. And just like the plant from which the book takes its name, each poem blooms with paradox: delicate and enduring; simply designed yet emotionally complex. Even though ghosts of grandmothers, mothers, wives, daughters, aunts, and sisters travel through dreams and darkness when the flowers close, and even though *I am a woman in an inkwell, drowning / because she did not answer me, Bloodroot* pulls down strength from the sun and sinks it into its juiced-red roots. Morse doesn't obscure the shimmering details of pain, but names and wonders and challenges. In doing so, this sharp poet transforms memories of abuse and regret into art."

-Christine Stewart-Nuñez, South Dakota Poet Laureate and author of *Bluewords Greening* (Terrapin Books, 2016)

More praise for Carmel L. Morse:

"In Bloodroot, Carmel Morse's poems capture the experiences and the people that have shaped her life. The poems are made of concrete words and images. They also have a deeper level that captures the emotional and spiritual depth at the root of the experiences. The first poem, "Onyx," is charged with striking images and it tells a story. The father rejects his child because it is a girl; however, he gives the narrator a beautiful necklace. Sixteen years later, when she prepares to deliver her second child, the father cannot accept that the baby is a girl. He leaves no gift and two years later he leaves for good. The narrator's life is so hard she almost sells the necklace, but she cannot. In order to remain strong, she *would unwrap the necklace/from the tissue paper/and fondle the stone.* Here is Eliot's Objective Correlative written with striking force, forging the experience in the reader's mind."

> –Gary Pacernick, author of *Memory and Fire: Ten American Jewish Poets*
> (Peter Lang, 1989)

Bloodroot

Poems by Carmel L. Morse

Luchador Press
Big Tuna, TX

Copyright © Carmel L. Morse, 2020
First Edition 1 3 5 7 9 10 8 6 4 2
ISBN: 978-1-952411-10-6
LCCN: 2020937847

Cover and title page image: Traci Grodner
Author photo: Traci Grodner
All rights reserved. No part of this publication may be reproduced or transmitted in any form or by any means, electronic or mechanical, including photocopying, recording or by info retrieval system, without prior written permission from the author.

Acknowledgments:

"Art Lesson with Aunt Emma" was published in *Fairfield Review* in 2006. "Boogie Woogie" and "Phonograph" were published in *Connecticut Review* the spring of 2010. "Menopause Dream" was published in *The Great American Poetry Show.* "Knowing Her" was published in *Aji Magazine,* Fall 2019.

TABLE OF CONTENTS

Onyx / 1

Love Child / 4

Second Marriage / 6

Stripped / 8

Rubella / 11

Menopause Dream / 12

Let Me Introduce You / 14

Mom and I Batchin' It / 16

Home Schooling / 18

Retrograde / 20

Acts of Contrition / 22

Calliope / 24

A Stitch in Time / 27

A Wing and a Prayer / 30

My Grandson Rides to Join Us / 31

Ghost Insomniacs / 33

Staples / 35

Body Work / 37

Early Departure / 40

Jetstream / 43

Boogie Woogie Nights / 45

Aunt Emma's Magic Show / 46

Knowing Her / 48

Phonograph / 49

Photo Opportunity / 51

Art Lesson with Aunt Emma / 52

Tuning In To You / 53

Bloodroot is dedicated to D. Scott Morse, my husband, and Theresa Jean Grodner, my daughter, who thankfully gave me the encouragement and space to realize my dreams. I also dedicate this to poets Sandra Feen and Holly Norton who provided loving and constructive feedback and advice on my creative writing throughout the years

This book would have not been possible without the women whose voices resonate in these poems – my mother, Billie Jean Garrett Lindgren; my sister, Greta Jean Lindgren James; my maternal aunt, Greta Emma Garrett Mackey; and my granny, Ida Fredericka Von Bargen Garrett.

A heartfelt thank you is also in order for the educators who were my mentors and editors throughout the past fifty years: Professor Hilda Raz, Dr. Gary Pacernick, Dr. Jerome Delamater, and in memory of Elene Anderson – my senior year high school English teacher who first referred to me as a *creative writer.*

-CLM

There is no greater agony than bearing an untold story inside you.

- Maya Angelou

Onyx
(Ida Von Bargen Garrett)

The German midwife
dipped rags in ice,
placed them on my forehead,
cheeks, neck, between my breasts.
I dug my fingernails
into the thin mattress,
smelled my sweat,
I thought I was dying.

Sixteen hours of labor
on a rainy March night
in 1899, in the bed
of our two-room apartment
near the railroad tracks.
I wailed loud as the train whistle,
then Emma entered the world.

When my breathing returned
to normal and Emma was swaddled
in pink cotton, Will came in. He frowned
at our baby, said, *Thought it would
be a boy. Next time, it's certain.*

He looked at the floor, handed me
a clumsily wrapped box he had hidden
behind his back. Inside, a black onyx

necklace, the filigreed chain black
with gold etching. It was the most
beautiful jewelry I had ever seen.

The midwife helped fasten it
around my neck, *Ah, onyx,* she said.
Gut. Means courage, strength.
Sometimes I wore the necklace
when I sewed or baked, to feel
the cool, smooth stone. It reminded
me of the refreshing ice
the night Emma was born.

Sixteen years later when I was with child
again, Will said, *It has to be a boy
with my name.*

When my time came and Will
heard the first cries, he rushed
into the bedroom before the cord
was cut, before I was covered.
Saw an absence, realized
we had another girl.

Will swore, took the Lord's name
in vain. *It's named William,
I don't care if it's a girl,*
he screamed, slammed the door,
didn't return for three days.
I named her Billie Jean. No
gift for my labors this time.

Two years later when Will
left for good, I could barely
scrape together enough
to feed my girls. Hard,
like onyx.
I almost sold the necklace,
but I needed it. Every day
when I scrubbed someone
else's floors on my hands
and knees, I needed to know
that I was strong,
and I would unwrap the necklace
from the tissue paper
and fondle the stone.

Love Child
(Billie)

A women with grey greasy hair
wearing a soiled apron
held me down.
The *doctor* had dirty fingernails.
When I screamed
the woman held a sweaty palm
over my mouth.
The pain was unbearable,
the doctor was rough,
his hands shook,
I saw the blurry blackness
descend like a matinee curtain
and passed out.
Then it was over.
The baby, created
from love,
was gone forever.

I stumbled out of the doorway,
into the brightness of Fisherman's Wharf;
the smells of the open markets made bile
seep into my throat.
The back seams of my stockings
were crooked, high heels caught
in the concrete as I steadied myself
holding onto the cracks
in the brick buildings.

I felt the warm trickle of blood
down my thighs,
pressed them together tight.

People passed by,
stared, left a wide berth,
whispered, *Drunk.*
But I kept moving,
there was no choice.
The darkness
swelled and dipped.
I could not faint.
The police would prosecute,
put Mother to shame.

Joe's family would kill me,
the ones who arranged the butcher,
the family that insisted on annulment,
the parents who made Joe
forget love, forget me.

Second Marriage
(Billie)

Jack was a charmer in those days –
Tall, slender, moved like Fred Astaire,
white-blonde hair and glacier blue eyes.
So debonair.
Tried to get in my pants on the first date.
I pushed him away, pointed to my
left ring finger, said
Fella, the store is closed
until this finger is filled.
He gave me a crooked smile
raised his right eyebrow.

We married ten days later
in Reno, his mother, Bertha,
as witness; she glared at me
throughout the two-minute
ceremony, surveyed me like a
piece of prime real estate.

I should've run like hell.

Jack was a salesman even then,
told me he was gonna make a killing
in life insurance or stocks or retail

and we'd live in the biggest house
on the tallest hill where green grass
would grow forever.
I bought the dream,
every spun sugar thread of it.

It was crazy love.

Stripped

You guard your secrets,
all the confusing middle-
of-the-nights you awake -
an empty pillow beside you.

The conflict, the wrongness
that appears as if a band
of steel is twisting
around your forehead,
drops of sweat bloom
on your upper lip
wetness wells under the chin,
the corner-of-the-eye teardrop,

I don't want to wake up.

This is the point where you
are still within reach of the gold
ring of sensibility on the whirling
merry-go-round,

Get out of bed!

Your legs won't move
in the house of crooked cards
demolished in a whisper,

Something is wrong.

You scramble for the bottle
of phenobarbital, take two,
wash them down with
diluted scotch and melted ice cubes
clutch the sheets, pull them
up to your neck, tight
as a mummy casing
and force your eyes closed.

I'm too tired.

Teardrops have made the sheets
smell of slight mildew,
damp basements,
and other problems absent
from your clean suburban home.

I mustn't think.

You remember as a young girl
the only thing that mattered
was the new linen skirt
Granny sewed for you
for the May Day Dance.
Back then there were no
men in the house, no evil
to ponder upon the vacant pillow.

The house is too damned quiet.

You hear the second hand counting
time on the bedside table.
You focus on small sounds,
your daughter's muffled cry,

No!
a door squealing
a lock clicking,
the shuffle of leather slippers.

You know that he
is returning to your bed
after visiting your daughter's,
but now your body floats in pleasant
warmth smearing all the other
feelings like thick frosting
on a cracked cake
and everything dirtied in the night
is clean again.

You decide to buy your daughter
a new spring outfit,
cambric skirt strewn with daffodils,
knife-edged accordion pleats
and white cotton tights,
Mary Jane patent leather shoes.

It's so damned peaceful here.

Rubella

Mom drew the heavy drapes
extinguished the drench of daylight,
placed my Mickey Mouse sunglasses
on my nose and led me by the hand
to the living room sofa, hoping
a change of space would cure me
when the penicillin didn't.
She wrapped me in a white
woolen blanket, static electricity
surged from my hand to her fingers,
like the Creation of Adam,
and I was energized, extended
the time between bathroom trips
when I hugged the toilet's cool porcelain
and Mom trickled icy water
on my brow, baptizing my fever.

Menopause Dream

It comes every quarter like late
menstruation, a belated full
moon, a hollowness buried
in the gut. I see a pod

cocooned in flesh and blood,
layers peeling in time-lapse speed,
then a maroon vein bursts. Still birth
and blackness.

Only the heart flutters, skips
a beat then drops hollow
point bullets in my
stomach. *Uterus mortis,*

eggs shrivel into raisins baked
in the oven of half a century.
Grief spreads like nightshade,
its purple-veined bellies

choke the brilliance
from the burning bush.
This type of loss felt only
once before at my sister's death.

Awake at three a.m.
a single candle flame eclipses
the rim of my wine glass
just like the summer

sun halos on my daughter's
blonde hair. Why is one
child enough for thirty
years, and then is not?

Let Me Introduce You

You already know the famous ones –
Monroe, Garbo, Dickinson, Mead,
but I want to introduce you
to some women I know,
my women,
ones I obsess over,
visit in sweet dreams
and nightmares.

Some are tough,
molten 45 Colt revolver types,
yet others are pucker sweet
like saltwater taffy.

Women built on red
lipstick smears and false
eyelashes like black
widow spider legs.

Those who bite
their toenails,
wear platinum
fingernail polish,

henna their hair,
wear pincurls to bed,
backcomb six inch beehives,
weave braids, chignons.

Martinis-on-the-rocks drinkers,
coffee with two teaspoons sugar,
water, no ice,
or chamomile tea with honey.

Tall women, short,
busty, willowy. Women
with bony knees, and some
who wear support hose.

Women who play five-card stud,
lay 'em down every time,
or play Chutes and Ladders,
let their children win.

You can't tug their hair,
kiss their cheeks.
But catch the heat waves steaming
on the arid horizon or the mist
hanging over a lake at dawn –
look, here they are.
These women are built with words.

Mom and I Batchin' It

I prayed for Daddy to go
on business trips,
then it was just us girls.
In the evening we set out in her
mulberry Ford Falcon convertible,
named *Purple People Eater*,
drove over to Bob's Drive-In
for cheeseburgers on crunchy
French rolls, melted cheese
smothered the meat, topped
with garden fresh tomatoes.
The juices and seeds dripped
down our chins.
In the rearview mirror she
reapplied Redberry lipstick
and we cruised
to Boulton's Five and Dime.
She bought me glassine envelopes
stuffed with foreign stamps
for my collection.
Our final stop, the library
where I checked out
Agatha Christie mysteries
for bedtime reading.

At home, I spread out my new
stamps on the carpet, showed
her the prettiest ones,
triangles of flowers
from Monaco,
storybook characters
from Romania.
Some nights we cuddled
in a blanket, watched
Rita Hayworth,
Humphrey Bogart,
Loretta Young
on the late show.

Then, I slept with her
in the queen-sized bed,
her measured breathing
lullabied me to sleep.

Home Schooling

I'm fourteen and Mom has plans.
Honey, you will learn tennis
and we'll buy you some of those
cute little skirts that show just enough
of your butt when the wind blows.
Boys will gawk at you.

She spins me a frilly pink cocoon
out of her failed dreams,
draws blueprints in her mind
for the mousey-haired
knock-kneed kid changed into
a frosted blonde princess
with padded bras, anti-perspirant
and contact lenses.

Boys will take you to dances
and then you'll marry
(after a long engagement)
a doctor or lawyer.

She reads *Glamour*,
Studies the ads for bottles, creams,
face paint and girdles,
cloning herself into me.

You'll be a virgin, of course.
We're stronger than men
because we have a hold over them.
They want it.
They'll do anything.
Make them beg.
You won't like it, you know,
but pretend.

Under her guidance, I scoot all over
the apartment on my bony ass
because all men like tight asses,
and she balances a book on my head
I'd rather be reading.

Retrograde

I still yearned for childhood
staples of Ovaltine, Crayolas,
and pads of foolscap paper,
the surface I would tickle
with my fingertips, mesmerized
by the rough-hewn fragments
of embedded brown threads.

I was rough underneath,
behind the platinum lipstick,
and lacy cornflower hair bows,
white fishnet hose that barely rose
above the cotton mini skirt hem
that I perpetually tugged
in pretended innocence.

Inside I was a geisha
with Mary Jane shoes
who practiced sashaying
ass movements in my tight
hip-hugging bellbottom pants.
I wore a gold monogrammed pin
at my throat like a chastity belt
that screamed no admittance,
but I didn't mean it.

I prowled the downtown department
stores looking for eligible young men
to phone me, to fill the time
between listening to "Louie Louie"
on the stereo and clipping out *Sixteen*
centerfolds. I searched every store for blue-
lensed granny glasses and love beads
made of smooth wood and glass that prismed
the rainbow in the Saturday sun.

I spent at least an hour before leaving the house
building up bright blue eye shadow,
de-clumping mascara on my lashes
one by one, tweezing the wiry black hairs
between my eyebrows,
taking up the hem
one more inch on my op-art
go-go dress, the Mondrian stripe
bisecting my AA-cup breasts.

When I prowled, I wanted my perfection
to be noticed, admired, accepted.

But when the boys stared,
I tossed my long blonde hair,
turned away.

Acts of Contrition

I saw the photograph on TV
of Dr. Martin Luther King's black suit
crumpled on a Memphis balcony,
his security guard pointing
too late, and the live feed
of Bobby flashing his perfect smile
and a peace sign
at the Ambassador Hotel
in L.A. just minutes
before he hit the ground,
a scarlet thorny halo
spreading under his head.

Although I prayed all night
for Bobby to live,
he died anyway.
Believe in nothing
and the heart doesn't bleed.

The wild courage
to take a stand
at fourteen was vital.
Sent all my allowance
to an anti-war group,
refused to smile for months,
wore at least six strands
of homemade love beads,

flashing them in indignation
at the bigots down South
who laughed at violence.

What else can a fourteen-year-old do
when the world fires pot shots,
and nothing is sacred,
but everything scars?

Calliope

She is Great-Granny, Aunt,
Sister and Mom.
She either hugs me into an asthma attack
or locks me in the coat closet.

I can't always see her
through clouds of smoke spiraling
from her three-inch ruby-studded
cigarette holder but

other times I see her clearly
in the sunlight reflecting
off strings of carnival baubles
circling her throat.

Her limbs are spongy
like homemade pillows
stuffed with ripped panty hose
and chicken feathers.

She wears a poodle skirt,
black w/pink dog stuck
with silver sequins
or a muu muu drenched
in purple azaleas.

She laughs with her head
slung back like a gambler
taking whiskey shots.
Her voice is bubbling water
from an artesian well.

She keeps generations
of crimson fingernails,
strands of henna hair
in a silk bag on a chatelaine
around her waist.

She presses rose petals
in a Woolworth's scrapbook.
Calls it *art.*

She swoons over Bogart
on the late-late show
(it's the way the word
Sweetheart whistles
through his front teeth).

She sneaks out at night.
skinny-dips
in the cemetery goldfish pond.

She's clairvoyant.
Tells the future
from the position of an olive
in a martini glass.

She forces me to write:
I can't see beyond my dreams
on my best watermarked paper
that I rip into shreds
and scatter like dandruff
in the wastebasket.

But then she touches
the exact spot on my throat
where a mole was removed
and makes me weep in grief.

A Stitch in Time

October 1952

My thread is spun on the beach
at Carmel, California.
The sea slapping the shore
my life and your motherhood.
Threads grow quickly into thick strands,
embroidery, perfect running stitches
to meld me to your warm flesh.
We are bound
slave to slave
master to master
in the internal spinning,
a braid of fate and rhythm.

November 15, 1981

Your cancer ceases
along with your heartbeat.
You stare at me with widening eyes
a stricken animal on the freeway,
as your final breath
leaves your lungs,
your blood, the hospital room.

I stumble across the parking lot
as your breath fuses with the firmament
and I feel our strong weave unravel
as if clumsy thumbs pull at us unmercifully.
I stop, keen loudly at the starless sky
as if a shaman reaches through my chest,
yanks out my beating heart.

For years I pick broken threads
from my wound, wishing I could reconnect
their fragile sperm-like tails.
I want to re-stitch a pattern,
an arrangement of hydrangeas
or a fire-snorting dragon.

May 2018

The words I've been writing
cause me to awaken one morning
crying, *Mama!*
Our jagged threads shriveled
into cables of dried blood
and snapped off at the roots years ago
and we are well past the stage
of burnt offerings. But now
the stitches are being reattached
in the blood of my granddaughter,
the minutia of living particles
no thicker than mosquito legs.

Our stitching grows thicker
with every stanza I write,
like the altar cloths
embroidered with silk threads on black velvet
by Ursuline nuns in Quebec City,
every stitch the proclivity
of patience, penance and prayer.

And my inheritance,
the sturdy, stubborn ties
were only frayed, not broken.

A Wing and a Prayer

I am a worm in an inkwell, drowning,
because she did not answer me.
Why?
When I reached my hand to the heavens
I did not feel the searing heat
of her fingers an aura away.
Was she busy gathering martyrs
for the community bonfire?
Embroidering swords on St. George's vestments?
Making sacramental wine
out of Garden of Eden dew?
So much is expected of angels today
as eternity goes into overtime
and extra innings are projected.
St. Peter calls set point
and there she is - stuck with one wing
sprinting to my rescue, the other
protecting latchkey children
as they negotiate crowds
of school crossing guards
searching for candied apples
without worms.

My Grandson Rides to Join Us

A monitor drums out your heartbeat
in echoes of th-thump, th-thump,
as you ride towards us,
gallop into the brightness
on a wild, winged appaloosa
dappled and brave.
The wind of the outside world billows
the mane, tickles your cheeks,
tempts you nearer. Come. Come.
The hammered hooves strike packed sand.
It is a long ride that lasts ten hours
and more, even more.

The nurses check your progress
as time is calculated
only in hoof beats, still strong and measured.
Drops of blood from your mother's
womb dot the floor – rain-drenched
red clay that grows from the marrow
of ancestors, the jelly of breath and flesh
creates the outline of your chin and nose
and makes you one of us, yet also
you, only you, individual snowflake.

Another monitor records the flow
and ebb of contractions as you
scale one mountain, pause,

slide down on gravel to the bottom,
then prance up another peak.
The mountain range is an endless circle
that bands the turquoise medallion
of earth and sky you begin
to enter alone and naked.

So hard to relax your fisted fingers,
let go of the honeyed mane & silenced
silky blackness as your mother grunts
you into the intense lights and stainless
steel-on-steel music. You squint,
mouth sucking emptiness,
experience the divine mystery

of skin touching skin,
then an aria of warbled cries
singing both mourning and joy,
convey your awe & confusion,
celebrate the epiphany of your life-breath.

Ghost Insomniacs

The clock reads 12:48 a.m.
Rudi the dog rests her head
on my ankle, her breathing
comes in tiny snorts
like air through a tin horn,
my eyes are open wide
in a barn owl stare.
Ghosts are visiting again.

I feel Mom tucking me in bed
under crisply ironed sheets,
safe, secure from dark.
I hear Greta's laughter
like tubular bells
in a March breeze,
smell Auntie Emma
cooking Spanish omelets,
the scent of onions and jalapenos
mingle with her Tabu cologne.

My senses reconstruct
as my brain deconstructs
in the pre-sleep pinnacle of night.
The clock hands drip minutes
in a Salvador Dali daze.
I feel craziness approaching,
climb out of bed, steal

downstairs, grab my journal,
pour a glass of Pinot Noir,
try to put my ghosts to rest,
tuck them between the crisp
pages and straight lines,
sheets pulled tight
under their chins.

Staples

> *"Self-harm" refers to the deliberate, direct destruction of body tissue that results in tissue damage . . . Several studies have found that individuals who engage in self-harm report unusually high rates of histories of childhood sexual abuse, childhood physical abuse.*
>
> – Red Rock Counseling, Colorado

Staples are necessary –

a handful of grain to grind into flour,

fresh milk to age into cheese,

churn into butter.

But I prefer the staples that attempt

to gather my loose ends,

the tiny steel jaw that pierces paper,

folds back over itself in tiny, clasped hands.

One link on a chain.

Pierce. Kachunk. Repeat.

Remove the staple

and the world becomes chaos,

papers swish to the carpet,

words flutter away,

paragraphs sever as I tenaciously bend

the steel fingers flat as a pin

creating a tiny stiletto

to stab at my forearm

then pull the steel shard

downwards towards the wrist.

Repeat.
It plows furrows in virgin skin.
Repeat.
I watch the blood bubble to the skin
like precious scarlet oil,
feel the flash point of pain.
Repeat.

This office staple becomes a feral animal
with pointed teeth stuffed with skin and blood.
Twenty crimson streams flow into my hand,
circle my fingers, pool in the cuticles,
this fire helps erase the blaze ignited by Daddy
when I was eight and *no* didn't work.
Repeat.
Kachink.
Repeat.

Body Work

I.
Our body temple is in perpetual
evolution, reparation, eventual
deconstruction all due to a tenet
of beauty as surface perfection

defined by media as gaunt,
full-lipped provocative,
skin bronzed like a basted
roasted goose.

Crooked noses, lined foreheads,
jutting chins, breasts like bean
bags tossed into the
eager mouths of plastic surgeons

who transubstantiate the multi-
grained doughy bread of self
into the flawless body.

II.
When I was eight Mom said,
> *Sweating is not lady-like.*
> *Don't let me catch you coming*
> *in perspiring like a boy.*

Mom never sweated.

Kept a machine by her bed;
red wires snaked from a metal
box, attached electrodes
to her stomach, abdomen, thighs.
She set it on high. Humming like
hives of bees, the box sent shocks
forcing muscle contraction. A
hundred stings pierced the skin
every ten seconds. Pain showed
in Mom's clenched teeth;
her fingers grabbed handfuls
of the bedspread.
> She explained, *This is what women do
> to keep their men happy.*

III.
Father, the cause of Mom's daily
shock treatments, bullied his sweating
body into my childhood bed at night.
Grinding pain like battery
acid stripped my feelings clean.
I sliced, scratched, gouged
my skin just to feel the sharp sting
of life. Scar like a tattoo
of a white leech
etched on my forearm.

IV.
When Mom died, fifty-pound shell
ravaged by cancer, skin stretched
taunt as onion paper over her bones,
no machines could transform her,
no man could demand perfection.

V.
Whether it's grinding of muscle
against tendon, tendon against bone
in the gym or slicing the abdomen
with a razor to experience
the bright flow like grenadine
circling the waist,
self-mutilation catches up with us.

VI.
We are good to our bodies in death.
Dressed in Sunday best, the dead
lie in pillowed, satin-lined
coffins, more elegant than the
marriage bed.

All body work comes down
to this: As soon as we are lowered
into the ravenous earth,
perfection becomes myth,
skin sloughs from our
skeletons like tissue paper
wrappings left in the rain.

Early Departure

Flying from Indy to Little Rock
yellow fluorescent stickers on my luggage:
> "LATE CHECK-IN"

accuse me as being a dawdling, unorganized traveler
as I rush to your home.

You have been
in a coma for three days,
finally free from the cancer pain,
crisp floral sheet folded and
tucked under your chin,
your face now void of worry.
You are still beautiful with
turned-up nose, cupid lips.
I grasp your cool, dry hand.
> *Greta, I'm here.*

Only your low snoring responds.

Can't think of what to say but feel
that if I can just find magical words
you will open your eyes and say
> *Hi Sweetie.*

So for some reason I sing
the bath song you used to sing to me when
I was four:
> *Carmie, where are you going?*
> *upstairs to take a bath*

> *with legs just like toothpicks*
> *and a neck like a giraffe.*

Your husband enters the room,
squints at me like I'm insane
and goes to nap after being awake
for the past twenty hours.
Sorrow has carved new
crevices on his face.

I caress your hand, your long fingers
that diapered me, dressed my dolls
when I was so young.
The hands that placed the bridal veil on my head,
brushed the tears from my cheeks when I divorced,
gripped my hand like a vice

when we watched Mom
also dying from cancer
strangle her last breath.
Now, your hand is still,
fragile porcelain.

    I sit with you until twilight.
Hospice nurse Patti arrives.
I am thirsty, lay your hand on the sheet,
take seven steps to the refrigerator.
    (six seconds)
Open the door, remove
two liter bottle of Diet Coke,
set it on the counter.

       (four seconds)
Come quickly, Patti demands
I rush to your bedside.
       (two seconds).
She is listening, stethoscope at your chest
smiles sadly, shakes her head.

In twelve seconds
you have left so quietly
I did not hear the wings come for you.

Jetstream

Last night I slept on sheets
worn soft as feathers, went
to a family reunion. Mom, Aunt
Emma, and Granny were there.

But you've all been dead for years,
I cried. They couldn't hear and kept
chatting about omelet recipes,
family pets, their laughs light as

salt rising biscuits. They changed
beds, sheets glided down
like gulls. The rest of the family
would be flying in.

I asked Mom when my older
sister would arrive. She frowned,
folded a perfect hospital corner,
Don't be silly. Greta's dead.

I opened my mouth but my
tongue expanded like a lung.
I couldn't reply,
But she died years after all of you.

I ran outside to autumn air,
stared at the sky, searched
for jets descending . Felt
a separation like water

evaporating from land. I flew
just as I did in childhood
when I had a fever
and the earth dropped

into midnight caverns studded
with flares of broken stars. Then
Greta arrived, her nurse's
uniform bleached to bright.

She grinned, moved a few steps
toward me, reaching out
to a hug, then suddenly
paused, twiddled her

fingers in a *toodle-loo* wave,
spun around, glanced over
her shoulder, merged with a
canyon of cumulus clouds.

Fevered and damp, I awoke
stunned by the yellow daylight,
jet engine shattering the sky.

Boogie Woogie Nights

May, 1942 you sang
at the Hilo Yacht Club,
war blackout nights
with the Glen Miller Wannabe Band.
You were bits of drama,
like Barbara Stanwyck,
but mostly Maxine, the Andrews Sister,
beautiful brunette with a long nose.
Your white teeth bright
in the hot spotlight.
Sing, Billie, sing.
You bellowed boogie woogie,
and a bit of be-bop,
your hips shimmied
as the notes slammed
from the staccato sax,
driving a wave of starched shirts
and satin swirls
onto the dance floor.

Auntie Emma's Magic Show

You are a rotund, robust,
rockin' and reelin'
kind of woman.
Not afraid to dangle your cigarette holder
in one hand and gather children
to your ample bosom with the other.

You smell like lavender sachets, patchouli incense,
raspberries and cream, and Tabu cologne
dabbed carefully on your pulse points.
Some looked at you and saw a woman
who let her looks go but I see
a theatrical production.

You wear Uncle Aubrey's raccoon coat,
strum his ukulele, make up lyrics
that include *Oh you, kid,*
and *Twenty-three skidoo,*
hike your quilted bathrobe up
to dance the Charleston –

It's in the knee action,
the bee's knees, you chuckle.

Your white sofa becomes the backdrop
for a drama from a roaring twenties
party replete with deeply dyed oriental carpets,

tarot card readers, and a metaphysical dynamo,
a mysterious man who plays perfect
Stravinsky on the Steinway
even though he never played a note before.
And the bathtub overflowing with gin, of course,
dozens of shiny Model A's with the dazzling
whitewall spare tire mounted on the side
lined up nose to bumper like well-trained
elephants on your circular driveway.

Your stories are the bunny
in the top hat, the dove disappearing
at the click of a wand, endless links
of silk handkerchiefs pulled from a cuff.
These are the tales that make me smile,
open my jaw in disbelief, imprison my eyes
behind my fingers, dissolve into giggles.

It is Aunt Emma's memory trunk
of vaudeville white rabbits that makes me vow
to learn the Charleston so I can dance
at my granddaughter's birthday party.

Knowing Her

It is an unexplainable sixth sense
traveling in matrilineal conduit,
sparks of knowing passing
in utero through the mother
to the daughter to the granddaughter
and on and on, spiraling
a flawless coil in time.

The spark a musical note,
in the umbilical cord
creating one perfect tone, a pitch
so pure it is like purified water
through a siphon singing the blues.

Each heartbeat thuds,
tightening ligaments
like a guitar string tuned
to high C that the daughter
hears through the catacombs
of arteries in the womb every time
her mother moves her hips,

a cradle like the faultless arc
of a dreadnought guitar, bowed,
fertile, woman-curved, perfection
of a plump moon.

Phonograph

When Big Sis left home
she gave me her song machine –
rock n' roll cranker,
played 45 platters
in stacks of five
like piles of flapjacks
on Saturday morning.

I clicked on the knob,
tubes re-born, hummed
a crackling overture,
reminded me of rustling
crinoline petticoats
when Sis practiced dancing
with her girlfriends after school,
perfecting the stroll
in our basement rec room.

My forefinger scraped
grey dust off the needle,
created a brief thunder of
hum and rasp
as the record floated down
like a parachute.

Black, baby blue, orange, red
labels swirled like pinwheels
identified legends:

Buddy
        Elvis
                Rickie
                        Fats
names as slick
as the shiny black plastic
that preserved their voices.

I lay my hand flat
on the hardwood floor.
Beats traveled up my arm
into my veins,
vaccinated me
with rock n' roll.

Photo Opportunity

Wearing black tights and
white leather boots
(a blithe musketeer),
I leap up on his
avocado kitchen counter
settling next to my saber,
a long carving knife.

Winking at him
I steal an orange
as incense/reefer/cigarette
smoke hovers overhead
in grey confetti haze.

The toaster reflection
makes my face fat
as I bite into the fruit.
It spits on my cheek.

He snaps a Polaroid picture
which develops in green, red streaks
like Christmas wrappings
in a rainstorm.

Art Lesson with Aunt Emma

On her patio in Salt Lake,
we squeezed pimples of cadmium
red, yellow ochre and cobalt blue
from tubes vivid as cartoon toothpaste.
Emma tossed me a sable hair brush, said,
> *Your creativity is a gift. Use it!*

Emma's house dress, smothered
in passion fruit flowers and hula
dancers, caressed her chubby knees.
Wearing red silk slippers she scuttled
like a Japanese Beetle between her easel
and scotch-on-the-rocks, the young flapper
still visible in her cropped henna hair,
baby-doll pink cheeks, crimson lips.

The Beatles sang "When I'm 64"
on the transistor radio. Emma cried:
> *Geez, I love that song!*
danced around patio chairs,
one hand on her waist, other hand
waving a brush, splattering paint
like ruptured maraschinos
on the concrete.

Tuning In To You

When the pavement rolls
into a shushed blackness
and the street sleeps fitfully
waiting for the occasional
rush of rubber
it's then I can tune in your voice
like a transistor radio
between border stations,
nine volt battery juicing out.
Outside the chalk clouds
swoon, scratching notes
of your songs across
the blackboard sky.

Carmel L. Morse earned a Ph.D. in English with a concentration in creative writing, poetry from the University of Nebraska – Lincoln. She also holds a graduate certificate in women's studies from Wright State University. She has been published in *Aji Magazine* (2018), *Connecticut Review* (Spring 2010), *Darkling* (2009), *Pudding Magazine* (2007), *Fairfield Review* (Editor's Choice Award, 2006), *Nexus* (2002, 2003), *Flights* (2000). She is the recipient of the Karen Dunning Award in Women Studies from the University of Nebraska for Branches, an illustrated collection of poetry, and earned a Certificate of National Merit (2nd Place, Poetry) from the League for Innovation in 2000. Dr. Morse teaches English, literature, and communication courses at the University of Northwestern Ohio in Lima.

www.ingramcontent.com/pod-product-compliance
Lightning Source LLC
Chambersburg PA
CBHW030138100526
44592CB00011B/940